5 Low Cost Business Ideas for Work at Home Parents

Book 4 in the '5 Simple Money Machines' Series

By

L J Samuels

No part of this publication may be reproduced, stored in a retrieval system or transmitted in any form or by any means, electronic, mechanical, photocopying, recording or otherwise, without prior written permission.

Please note that much of this publication is based on personal experience and anecdotal evidence. Although the author and publisher have made every reasonable attempt to achieve complete accuracy of the content in this book, they assume no responsibility for errors or omissions. Also, you should use this information as you see fit, and at your own risk.

Any trademarks, service marks, product names or named features are assumed to be the property of their respective owners, and are used only for reference. There is no implied endorsement if we use one of these terms.

Nothing in this guide is intended to replace common sense, legal, medical or other professional advice, and is meant to inform and entertain the reader.

Finally, there are no guarantees that you will make any money at all; your own efforts will determine your own results. *This book intends to show what is possible.*

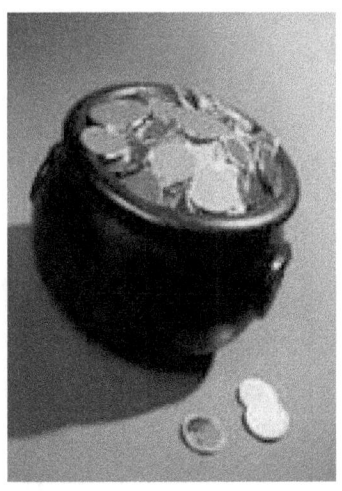

After reading this book you will have 5 more systems for putting money in your bank, time and time again, month after month. This time we are looking at simple ways to make money for the Work at Home Mom – or Dad.

"People who think money can't buy happiness just don't know where to shop…" ~ *Unknown*

Contents

Introduction	5
Method 1	15
Method 2	19
Method 3	33
Method 4	40
Method 5	44
Bonus Method 1	48
Bonus Method 2	50
Bonus Method 3	53
My Final Thoughts	55

5 Simple Money Machines for the Stay at Home Mom (or Dad)

Introduction

Welcome to Book 4 in the '5 Simple Money Machines' Series.

In this book you will learn 5 Simple Money Making Methods that you can comfortably work from home whilst being there for your children.

When my own children were small I would have loved the opportunity to be at home with them to see the milestone events such as first step, first smile etc. but, at that time, I didn't have any idea about the online opportunities that existed.

As a Dad of 4 daughters, I was under the mistaken impression that I could only provide stability and a good standard of living for my family by working for a boss.

I was WRONG!

I now know different.

Working from home can be very lucrative if you know how to go about it.

In the beginning I spent a lot of my spare time learning all I could about internet marketing. It was over two years before I was making enough money online to quit my 'day job' in order to scale up my business.

You can work from home too if you are willing to learn and put in some time and effort.

Please don't give up at the first hurdle - persistence pays.

This book will show you 5 different methods to kick-start your online money making journey.

I really hope you will stick with it long enough to make enough money to give your family lots of the little extras that make life so much more exciting.

The work required to implement these systems is simple, quick and even a person with only a basic understanding of internet marketing could begin to make money with the right guidance.

In fact some of the methods don't require that you use the internet at all unless you need to scale up and market your product or service to a wider audience.

I will do my best to lay out these systems in an easy-to-understand way but, if you need any help at all, please send me an email to the address at the end of this book and I will do my best to help you get up and running making money from home.

As I have said before (I do tend to repeat myself...) in Book One of this series

"5 Simple Money Machines that Pay You Over and Over – After Doing the Work **JUST ONE TIME**",

And in Book Two

<u>5 MORE Simple Money Machines that Pay You Over and Over - **For Very Little Work!**</u>

And, yet again in Book Three

<u>5 Simple **OFFLINE** Money Machines that Pay you Over and Over</u>

(If you are interested in any of the first three books in this series, simply type the word that are underlined into Amazon's search bar)

I am basically a lazy person and now find it reasonably easy to make a living by working hard for a while then kicking back and watching the money come in.

This time we will be looking at different ways to create a few income streams that can make you a very nice bit of cash without having to go out of the home to work.

We will be concentrating on methods that you can implement whilst still being there to look after your children.

Can I just add that the first three books in the '5 Simple Machines' series also contains some great ideas that parents working from home could utilise to make extra cash.

With this book I have listed *even more* great and 'doable' ideas.

Note: I will use the term 'Work at Home Mom' or WAHM a lot in this book but the information could (and does...) also apply to Dads.

Working at home requires a different attitude than going out to work for a company.

When you work outside the home for someone else, you will have to keep to their timetable and rules. Your job will be structured to fit in with the requirements of the company.

Working at home means that you can set your own timetable, decide if you want to work five days a week or less and you can decide to take a break when you want to.

However, to make the best of a work at home opportunity it is best to have your own structure in place where you have times that are 'work' times.

If you have school aged children you could set aside a couple of hours in the morning after they have gone to school or even late evening when they are in bed.

The great thing about working at home is that you get to decide what works for you and your family situation.

What Makes a Successful Work at Home Mom (or Dad)?

What are mornings like in your house – chaotic, stressful, frantic and noisy?

I bet it is all of these things if you have a couple of kids to get ready for school before dashing off to your own nine to five.

Wouldn't it be great to be able to get out of bed, get the children off to school and then work at home, instead of the usual crazy commute?

Well, guess what – with careful planning you could work at home and be your own boss and timekeeper. There would be no-one to tell you what time to start work or what time to go home; no-one to tell you when you can take a break etc.

It would all be up to you.

In order to be a successful work at home mom you will need to be just as organized as you were when you had to go out to work.

If your work at home job is internet based you will need a place to work – the kitchen table is usually the place most of us find easiest.

Working in your kitchen is great if you have a toddler because you can still keep an eye on him whilst you do some work.

A good idea would be to have a set time during the day or evening that is 'work' time.

I work best in the early mornings and late evening so I have two hours between 9am and 11am that is my work time and again at 9pm to 11pm.

But you have to be disciplined in order to do the best job you can in the shortest time possible.

You shouldn't put off your work to do the ironing, play a quick video game or watch a TV program – you will find yourself getting stressed and playing 'catch up' if you get behind in your work.

When it is time for work, switch off the phone, the TV, your instant messages etc. and concentrate your mind on your work.

There are tons of online opportunities for work at home moms, so spend some time browsing online and checking out what there is available.

10 Bizarre Business Ideas That Made Millions

http://youtu.be/WBe9lyv6U_g

Have a look at the video above – there are some really crazy ideas that have made their creators loads of money. The only limit to how you can make money and how much you can make is your own imagination and self-imposed limitations.

You have to believe in yourself; know that you can and will set up your home business and make it successful.

If the first thing you try doesn't make you any money within a month or two – move on to the next. Eventually you will find the perfect way to make that extra cash.

Whatever you choose to do to enable you to work at home, try to make it something you enjoy doing.

You'll be surprised at how quickly the time passes if you are enjoying your work. It may take a few months or so to get yourself established doing whatever it is that you've chosen to do; but after that you should begin to see some great returns for your efforts.

In my opinion, there is nothing quite like being able to bring in some extra cash whilst still being available to do the school run or being at home to see all the new stuff your toddler is learning.

That is the pleasure of being a parent

Contrary to some of the internet marketing hype that you see everywhere, there are no instant or 'push button' money makers. But the WAHM (Work at Home Mom) has lots of opportunities to make some extra cash for the household.

It may take a little time before the money starts coming in, but it will – if you are consistent.

Again, as in the first three books in this series, these methods should only take around an hour or two each day, so you should still have the time to do your normal household chores and as well as some fun stuff like taking the kids to the park.

As before, these methods are scalable, which means that you can add to them and increase the frequency you do them allowing you to increase the amount of money you receive each month.

The text below is in all of the first three books in this series and is just as important in this case…

> "…I urge you to remember that you will only get out what you put in.
>
> What I mean by that is, if you read this and think; "that's great, I can do that", then you do absolutely nothing; that is exactly what you will get back – **a big, fat NOTHING!**
>
> Again, can I take the time to stress that you have to make sure that each method you tackle is your **very best work**.
>
> Throwing together an incomplete, untested or badly written product, sales page, advertisement or email will not produce the results that you want – so make it the very best that you possibly can!"

Right, let's get to it…

Method 1

Portrait Photography Business

With all the possible contacts that stay at home parents have, this method could prove very lucrative indeed.

Everyone loves a good family portrait or photographs of the children to hang on their wall or to add to the family album.

You are in a perfect position to take advantage of this.

If you have a good quality camera you can take family portraits for others. You could do a few sessions for friends and family at a reduced cost then invest your profits into some professional equipment – it should only cost a few hundred dollars.

It will pay you to invest in a good background cloth and some simple lighting equipment in order to produce top quality portraits. If you don't have the money available in the beginning, you could use a white bed sheet as the backdrop and take your photos outside when the light is at its brightest.

Once you have taken your photos you could easily transfer them to some of the great fantasy digital backgrounds that are available.

This could be your unique selling point (USP).

You may want to spend some time learning a bit about enhancing images so you can provide your clients with the very best portraits.

A good place to learn how to do anything these days is YouTube.

After a simple search, I found this video that shows how simple it is to take an image that has been shot on a white background and insert it into a really cute background with Photoshop.

How To Remove A Background For Digital Backgrounds And Props Using Pho...

http://www.youtube.com/watch?v=3S270NXZCGU

(I am not affiliated in any way with this website but just thought it a good instructional video that may help you)

If you don't have Photoshop, you can download and use a free photo editor. Search on Google for GIMP, download for free, then watch some of the many YouTube tutorials on how to use it. It is really easy when you get the hang of it.

There are lots of websites where you can purchase the fantasy backgrounds to edit your photographs on to.

I began by taking photos of my own children and inserting the pictures on to a couple of different backgrounds. Then I had the resulting pictures enlarged and framed so I had some samples to show to my prospective clients.

Advertise in your local free newspaper and put a poster on the school and church noticeboards. Chat to other Moms and Dads when you pick up the kids from school telling them about your new venture.

Have some leaflets printed – don't forget to include your sample pictures so people can see what you do.

Also include a price list for 'entry level' photographs, making it very clear that for large photos, special backgrounds etc. there will be extra charge.

If you know lots of people with young babies, why not have an afternoon 'party' where parents can bring their kids, have a chat and a coffee. You would then take some photos of the babies in front of your already set up white or green background.

Make sure your prospects know that the 'sitting' is free and they will only have to pay if they want the photographs.

Not many parents or grandparents will be able to resist the cute photos of their kids that you will easily be able to create using the fantasy backgrounds.

You only need to create the finished photo online, then edit it with a watermark so your clients will have to purchase from you to be able to use the photos.

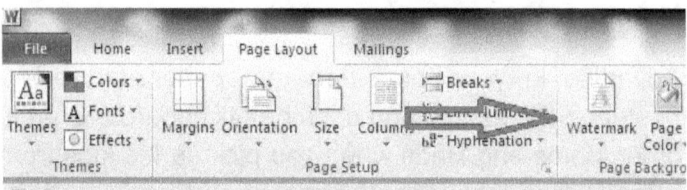

I paste the picture onto a Word document then add the watermark to the page.

Email the watermarked copy to the client and wait for the orders to roll in.

This business is a really good money spinner if you market it properly as the finished fantasy photos can command a very good price.

Method 2

Book Creating for Others

This method is something that really caught my imagination.

If you are a reasonable writer, can transcribe an interview or know someone who can, you can create a Family Legacy book for people who would like to record their memories and life experiences for their family to keep and cherish.

The book will be professionally published and bound for them to put on their bookshelf.

I still do this for the occasional client and I really enjoy listening to their stories. However, the best bit about doing this is watching their faces when you present them with finished copies of their beautiful book.

Don't forget most of your clients will have no idea how easy it is to self-publish these days. You are offering a unique service.

You will also be able to create books for fundraising, publish your clients own poems, manuscripts, recipes etc., create photograph books for 21st birthday gifts;

create personalised children's books etc., all in a professionally bound and printed book.

I started off my Family Legacy creating business with some great FREE advertising by holding a competition in conjunction with my local paper.

The entrants had to submit a piece not longer than 400 words saying why they should have a book published about their life or family.

The editor and I read all the entrants and chose a winner.

I then did that book for free. By doing this I was also able to calculate how long the process would take and it gave me a good idea how much to charge subsequent clients.

In the copy for the competition I outlined my new business; the Family Legacy books, the fundraiser books, the children's gift books, photograph books and the complete book compiling and publishing service.

This was how I secured my first three paying clients for the complete book writing service.

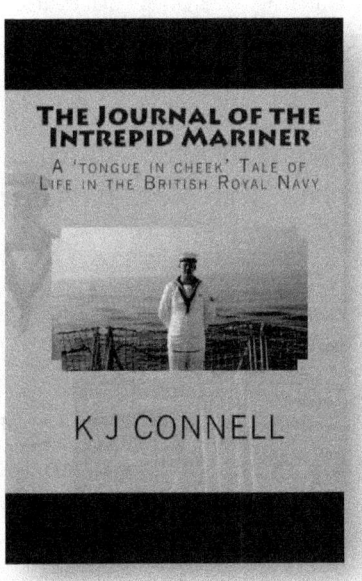

Above is a book created for a client using this method

So the one free book I did for the competition winner as a loss leader, really jump started my new business venture.

It also gave me an idea of the time involved when working for an individual client, so I was able to structure my pricing more accurately.

I realised that I needed a scale of charges according to the length of the finished book so I wasn't compiling a huge tome for the same price as a short book.

Once I have all the material collected I put it all together and format the book for publishing.

I used Createspace.com to publish my physical books. It is easy to upload books for publication and is free (my favourite price…☺), except for the small cost of a proof copy + p&p of around $10.

If you are familiar with self-publishing this should be easy for you.

If however, you have never done this before you will find below a very simple outline of self-publishing on Createspace.

The Self-Publishing Method

The first thing to remember is that this particular publisher will publish _EXACTLY_ what you send them.

So you need to format your pages correctly (I'll show you how…) and proofread it yourself or get someone else to have a look over it for you.

I usually finish a book, proof and edit it once, then put it away for a week or so before doing the same again. I also get someone else to go through it for obvious spelling and grammar mistakes.

It is amazing the simple mistakes that you will pick up after reading through a second time. There is nothing more frustrating than receiving your proof copy, only to find a very basic grammar or spelling error.

The first step, after you have written your book is to:

Sign up at Createspace

Visit the website www.createspace.com and sign up for a free account.

Simply follow the step-by-step process – it only takes a few minutes.

Formatting the Interior of the Book

I am going to tell you how I format my books before uploading them.

There are lots of other ways to achieve the same thing, but this is the one that I find is easiest for the beginner.

Once you are confident with this method of formatting your book, you could check out other ways to customize the size of your book.

The first thing you need to know is the size that you want your finished book to be. There are a number of standard industry trim sizes available from 5" x 8" to 8" x 10" and sizes in between.

I use the 5.25" x 8" trim size for most of my books because it makes it easy to use a standard Word document for the draft.

To begin, open a Word document and write your working title.

On your toolbar go to "Page Layout", from there choose the "Size" option. Select the 'custom' or 'more paper sizes' option in the dropdown menu and type in 13.4cm for 'width' and 20.4cm for 'height'.

Make sure 'apply to whole document' is selected, click OK and your page(s) will be re-sized automatically.

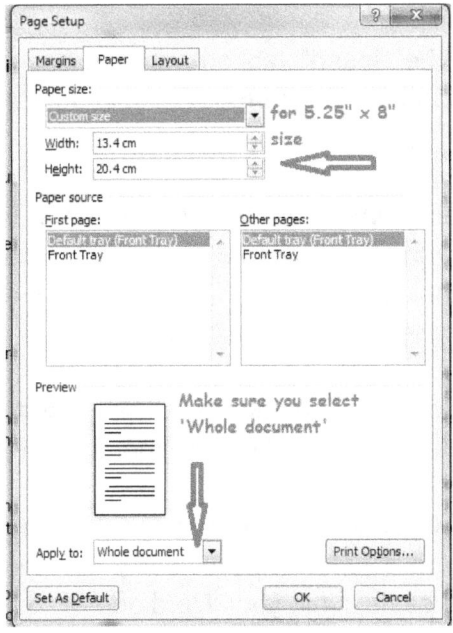

You can re-size a completed book this way, but you must make sure you go through the whole thing very carefully after you resize to make sure everything is positioned exactly how you want it.

Set the line spacing to 1.15 to make the book easier to read. I use 11pt and Arial font for my physical books; it is easy on the eye and looks good in print, but the choice is yours.

I usually add a 'footer' to my physical books (but not Kindle books) which includes the book title, copyright and page number.

Click on the "Insert" tab on your toolbar and select "footer". Choose the format for your footer from the dropdown list.

Write exactly what you want to appear at the bottom on every page. Centre it, then click "close" on the toolbar that popped up. Your footer should then appear at the bottom of each page.

Always add page numbers. Click "Insert" on your toolbar then "page numbers" on the dropdown menu.

Right, now you know how to do the preliminaries you are ready to collate your previously collected material to cut and paste it into your Word doc.

When everything is exactly as you would like to see it in your published book, turn the Word doc into a .pdf file by choosing 'save as' in the 'file' tab then choose the 'pdf option.

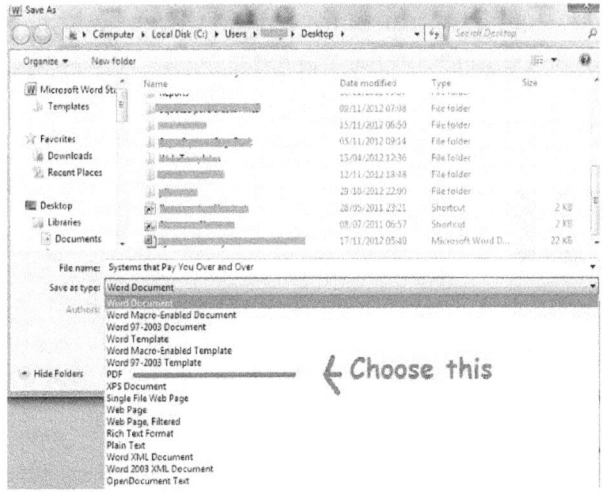

This .pdf file is what you will upload to Createspace.

The Book Cover

Next you need a cover for your book.

You could use the free cover design that Createspace offer, it allows you to change colours, fonts, add photos and descriptions etc. or you could find a good graphic designer to do this for you.

A good place to search for a good book cover designer is Fiverr.com. It will cost you – yup, you guessed it - $5!

There are some really good designers available. Just do a search for 'Book Cover' on Fiverr and see what comes up. Look for someone who has lots of good feedback and recommendations.

As you can see from the image above, there were 966 results when I searched for 'Book Cover Design'. I clicked on 'rating' to find the ones that had good feedback.

Next you should check out each 'gig' to see which one looks good to you.

(This is a book cover that was done for a Createspace book by someone on Fiverr – look s better in colour…)

Once you have got your interior 'pdf file and your book cover it's time to upload it all to Createspace.

Sign in to your account at www.Createspace.com and follow the simple instructions to set up the details for the new book for publication. Then upload your files as instructed (*when you are asked for the preferred book size, choose 5.25" x 8" if you have used the page sizing suggested above*).

If you run into any problems, Createspace have excellent customer service and a quick phone call or email will usually answer all your questions.

Alternatively, you can shoot me an email (address at end of this book) and I will do my best to help.

Once you have uploaded your files, you need to wait until you get an email telling you they have been approved.

Go back to your Createspace account and order a proof copy; it will cost around $10 including p&p.

When it arrives, check it carefully to make sure everything is exactly as you want it to be and check it very carefully for spelling and grammatical errors.

You don't want to present your client with a book containing mistakes.

If your book does need any revisions, correct it within your source file then re-save as a .pdf as above and re-upload your file to Createspace as before.

Order another proof copy to make sure that everything is fine.

Once your book is exactly as you want it to be, click the 'publish' button on your Createspace book page if your client wants the book to be available for general sale.

The book will be on Amazon for anyone to purchase for as long as your client chooses to leave it there.

That's it – you're done!

I usually present my clients with 3 copies of their book as part of the 'package'.

This has the potential to be a very lucrative business if you like to meet and chat to people.

Try chatting to the residents at your local care home for the elderly – they usually have some really interesting stories to tell.

Many would love the opportunity to publish their memories in a book that could be read by their whole family.

There is a book that describes the whole Family Legacy method along with all the information you need for uploading to Createspace and also instructions for uploading to Amazon Kindle if your client would like you to.

It also has a good section on using your skill to create a workshop business teaching others your new skill.

Here is the Kindle version

http://www.amazon.com/dp/B0078Y5VMI

Here is the physical book version

http://www.amazon.com/dp/1470089521

(If you are in UK, simply change .com in the link to .co.uk)

Method 3

Crafts

If you have a talent for making anything or you know lots of others who do, you have the potential to make a very nice income.

With a bit of imagination I'm sure you could come up with lots of ways to make money with crafts.

To start you off here are 5 opportunities for the 'crafter' or crafters friend to try. You could set up a few of these methods to maximise your potential income.

1. Set up an Online Store to Sell your Crafts

You could set up a store selling your crafts at www.Etsy.com or www.Dawanda.com

These are great places to sell your stuff as you don't need a domain name or hosting, you simply set up your own sales pages listing your products within the website.

The cost to you is minimal; usually a listing cost plus a percentage of the sale price. But if you products are good sellers, you can easily make a very nice profit.

Check each site to see their charges.

You can list your items on lots of different sites but be sure to remove them from all the sites they are listed on after they have been sold.

You can sell almost anything you make on these sites. From dog collars to man collars (☺) and headbands to headboards – you can sell it all.

Make sure you have some good photographs of your work to upload so it is displayed to its best advantage.

Be professional when dealing with online clients; they could become repeat customers.

It is advisable to have a Paypal account because this is the most popular method for paying for online goods and your customers don't want to have to jump through hoops to buy your stuff.

2. Sell the Craft Work of Others for a Commission

If you have friends that make things but don't know anything about computers, you could list their work on Etsy.com etc. for a commission.

My own mother makes beautiful decorated eggs; knitted children's wear and cross stitch but would have no idea how to go about selling them.

You could advertise your craft listing or selling services on the church noticeboard.

If you do sell other peoples crafts make sure you factor in selling costs when settling on a commission fee. There will be listing costs, Paypal fee etc.

If you are internet savvy, you could set up your own ecommerce website where you could list your own and other people's products.

You will need a domain name and hosting.

Using Wordpress, a free theme and free ecommerce plugin, it is really easy and very cheap to go down this route.

Spend time getting your website link out to as many places as possible to increase the internet presence of your new website.

Get lots of one way backlinks then, when you are getting lots of visitors to your site, you are ready to sell advertising space to other crafters.

You could charge a fee for others to list their products on your site.

You can list the products on Ebay. When you ship something you have sold, include a slip thanking your customer for their purchase and invite them to visit your website.

3. Craft Fairs

Craft Fairs are another great place to sell your wares. I know quite a few people who make a good living selling their work at Craft Fairs and local markets.

Search online for a list of upcoming Craft Fairs in your area. This is an excellent resource

http://www.artsandcraftshows-usa.com

…or for UK

http://www.ukcraftfairs.com

Again you could sell other people's crafts on your stall and charge a small commission per sale.

4. Craft Kits

You could construct some Craft Kits.

If you know where to get good quality, reasonably priced craft supplies you could put together some craft kits.

You can make a kit for any sort of craft from teddy bears to dolls houses and embroidery kits to children's wooden furniture.

If you know where to get jewellery supplies for instance, you could get together all the beads, wires, clasps etc. required to make a beautiful necklace with matching earrings, a bracelet or whatever.

Put it all together in a nice box with simple instructions and label it.

There are loads of people that would love to have everything ready prepared so they can just put the item together and still be able to say that they had made it themselves. These are very popular items to sell at Craft Fairs.

5. Craft Fair Organiser

Organise your own Craft Fairs. Find a venue that you can hire for the day, check out availability and cost.

It could be a room in a community centre, a room in a hotel or maybe your church has a room that you can hire. Make sure the room has enough space to have at least 20-30 stalls or tables to make the event attractive to sellers and buyers.

Charge per table and specify the **maximum size** of the table as some people will arrive with a *huge* table and expect to pay for one – there are chancers in all walks of life...

Advertise your event anywhere you can think of; free ad papers, craigslist, usfreeads, church notice boards, store notice boards etc.

Do lots of advertising because your clients will book with you again for any subsequent Craft Fairs you organise if you provide them with lots of potential customers.

Design a booking form and send it to anyone who expresses an interest. Make sure that you get at least 50% payment for each booking so you know they are not just 'tire kickers'.

On the day, you can have your own stall selling your crafts. You will save money by not having to pay for your own stall and at the same time, make a few dollars for everyone who books a space.

If you do not have anything to sell yourself, you could sell drinks and snacks to your stallholders and buyers.

The weeks coming up to the holidays will almost guarantee lots of potential customers as people are looking for unusual and beautiful gifts to buy. Make sure you book your venues well in advance as the best places are usually in big demand through the holiday periods.

Always take a booking fee for the holiday Craft Fairs and remember to do lots of advertising so you attract lots of potential customers for your stall holders.

Once you have a list of loyal crafters who book spaces regularly at your Craft Fairs, you could offer to organise Craft Fairs for school fundraising, church fundraising etc. for a small fee.

A lot of organisations would jump at the chance to have a professional organise their fund raising event. To raise money for the cause you could run a raffle and have spot prizes throughout the day.

When advertising, be sure to include the name of the charity that will benefit, as well as the prizes that are available on the day.

Your expertise and your list of potential stall holders will be a great selling point for offering to organise Craft Fairs for other organisations.

The organisation could have two stalls for free to sell their crafts to raise money and you could offer a donation to their cause.

Organising Craft Fairs can become a very lucrative home business if you put in the time and effort.

Method 4

Party Plan

Everyone knows about Home Party Selling through companies like Tupperware and Avon.

What about setting up your own Party Plan Company?

Simply source some good quality items that you know people will be interested in.

For example, candles, crafts, unusual gifts or you could even hold 'portrait' parties selling your fantasy photos as described in method 1.

Another party plan idea that gets lots of requests is a Pet Lover Party business. People buy all sorts of things for their pets, particularly dogs. You could sell dog and cat toys, pet clothing, grooming equipment, beautiful collars and leads, high end dog beds – the list is endless.

If you prefer, you would only need to buy one example of each product then, when your party guests have placed their order, you would buy only what is needed to fill the orders.

However, you may want to invest some money and buy a stock so you can actually sell your wares on the night. A lot of people prefer to go home with their purchases rather than pay first then wait for delivery.

Organize the first party in your own home inviting all your friends and their friends. From that first party you should be able to book parties at other people's houses and so on – you know how it works.

Offer a nice incentive to the host of the subsequent parties such as a percentage of the sales from their party.

This would encourage the host to invite guests that they know will be willing to spend money on the goods you are selling.

You could also offer a choice from a selection of gifts to the host for each future party booked at their party.

To avoid people receiving free gifts for cancelled parties, the gift they selected would be presented after each follow-up party. So, the first gift would be given after the first party that was booked from theirs, the second gift after the second party and so on.

This is a great way to get more parties booked; everyone encourages each other to hold a party to get free gifts.

Make sure to have some 'get to know you' games ready to break the ice.

Here are 2 deas to get you started.

1. Each guest has to state their name and tell everyone something that no-one else could possibly know about them.

2. Have a bowl of coloured sweets and a large sheet of paper with a list of 4 colours. Write a question next to each colour. For example next to the colour red, you could write "When was the last time you told a lie" and so on.

Without showing the paper to the guests, ask each person to take 4 sweets from the bowl (remind your guests not to eat them yet).

Now show them the paper and go round the room asking each guest to pick a colour of one of their sweets then answer the question on the list. Keep going until everyone has exhausted their supply of sweet.

This can cause great hilarity depending on the questions you have written down.

The sky's the limit with this home business idea.

You can employ other party organisers to demonstrate your goods, you can increase the type of parties available and let your next host choose what they think will sell well at their home party etc.

For instance, someone may have attended a 'Fragrance' party but know that a 'Pet Product' party would be best suited to their circle of friends. This is also a good selling point for your Party Plan business.

Important: *Never try to sell substandard products or your business won't last beyond the first couple of parties. Make sure everything you offer for sale is top quality.*

You will need to be very well organised to run a potentially fast growing business such as this. Keep a very accurate diary and order book. Collect payments with the orders and make sure everyone is happy with their purchase.

Customer service is very important in the Party Plan business. Going the extra mile for your customers will help your party plan business to stand out above the others.

Method 5

Simple Book Keeping for the Small Business Owner

This is another great earner because lots of small business owners get overwhelmed with the idea of keeping organised records and simply stuff receipts and invoices into a box then panic when it is time to do their tax returns.

You would offer to keep all their business records in order so when the year-end arrives everything is so much more easily put together for their accounts.

Each week or month you collect all their paperwork and spend a few hours recording it and putting all the receipts and invoices in order.

You would get invoices ready for payment, create the envelope and write the cheque ready for the client's signature. You would prepare the invoices for your client to send out to his customers.

The amount you could charge for this is really dependant on the amount of work each client requires; no two businesses require the same level of admin work. It would also depend on where you are in the world.

Doing this for one small business owner such as a plumber, electrician, builder etc., should only take, at the very most, an hour a week after you have done the initial organisation of their paperwork.

So you could make quite a nice monthly income by having around 10-20 clients.

Get some good business cards made and always keep some in your pocket to hand out when the occasion arises.

Put up posters in the local builder's merchants or in places where your potential clients will buy their materials, in the free ad papers, Craiglist, the church noticeboard etc. detailing your new book keeping service.

Once you sign up a client, ask if he can give you the names of some other small business people who may be interested in your service.

Offer one free months work in return for everyone you sign up from his recommendations.

This is a great way to get more business because everyone loves the idea of getting something for free and they will try their best to think of people to recommend you to.

You could also join the local Chamber of Commerce group and attend any networking meetings they arrange. Be sure to take a good supply of business cards to these events.

Get as many of the local newspapers as are available in your area and check out the 'services' section. Look for the 'one man' type of adverts and write down their details.

You will probably find that there are only phone numbers listed. So, if you are confident with the idea of speaking to a prospective client, give them a call and tell them what you do.

However, if cold calling is not your idea of fun, check out the Yellow Pages to see if you can find an address or simply ring and ask for a mailing address. Tell them that you want to send them a special/free offer.

Then put together a letter explaining what you do and offer to do two months work with one month free (3 months in total) if they pay in advance.

Fix your business card to the leaflet with a paperclip.

For those who don't get in touch, follow up with a phone call after a week or so asking if they got your letter.

Note: Don't offer to do the first month for free because this is when you have to do the most work setting up an organised system from your clients paperwork.

Once you have struck up a good relationship with your clients, there are lots of other things that you could offer to do for them to improve their business.

For instance, if they don't have a website, you could offer to do that for a fee.

You don't have to do this yourself; you simply outsource it and make a nice one-off fee simply for being the 'middle-man'.

A good website where you can outsource most things is www.odesk.com or www.elance.com

There will of course, be on-going costs for these extras to your client, such as maintenance of the website as well as the monthly hosting fee. You could charge a small fee to take care of this for them.

If they have a website that is nowhere to be seen in the search results, you could offer to help them get better search results by adding their business to Google Places etc. again, this work could be outsourced..

Again, the only limit to the services you can offer is your own expertise.

Read on for a couple of Bonus Methods.

Bonus Method 1

Sell Garden Plants

If you are a keen gardener you could sell your surplus plants.

When you plant seeds you will always get lots more seedlings than you can use. So, instead of tipping the extra seedlings onto the compost heap, pot them up into small cheap pots to sell.

What about when you have shrubs or herbs in the garden that need to be thinned out? Divide up the plants carefully and pot up the extra to sell on.

Herbs are easy to grow and are a great seller.

A lot of children would love to help with this type of enterprise and it will teach them a little about responsibility if they are encouraged to grow their own plants to sell for a bit of pocket money.

You don't need to have a huge garden to grow plants to sell. A few trays of seeds will produce masses of seedlings for you to pot on.

Where to Sell Your Plants

If there is a nursery close by, call in and see if they want to buy your plants. They usually have to buy quite large amounts of the same type of plants, so may be delighted to be able to buy a small amount at a reasonable price.

If you live on a busy street, set up a stall at the bottom of your drive. Get the children to help, most kids love to play 'shop'. You could even encourage your children to grow some plants of their own to sell.

Ask in your local store, a lot of stores sell plants and culinary herbs.

If you have a lot of healthy herb plants, ask around the local restaurants. A lot of chefs would be happy to buy your fresh herbs at a reasonable price.

Make up some hanging baskets to sell. They are always popular as it means the buyer can just take it home and hang it up.

This is a great way to involve the children in a profitable enterprise that most will love doing.

Bonus Method 2

Writing Opportunities

There are lots of opportunities for good writers. Here are two to get started.

If you can write a simple 300 – 400 word article you can make some extra cash by writing content for websites and blogs.

You don't have to be an expert in the subjects that you are asked to write about, just do a little searching online for other articles on the required subject.

For example, if you are asked to write about cooking for kids, type into Google, 'cooking for kid's articles' and you will be presented with tons of articles to give you your own ideas.

There are websites where you can advertise your services for free or very cheap, such as www.elance.com, www.digitalpoint.com and lots more.

If English is your first language and you can write a good, informative article, you will have as much work as you can handle. There are however, writers from Singapore, India etc, who only have English as a second language (and in many cases it shows…) that advertise their writing services for very little money – sometimes as low as $1 per article.

Do not try and compete with these writers on price. You would only be competing on quality of work.

Set a realistic starting price per article – maybe $1.50 per 100 words and stick to your guns on the price.

You will need some testimonials to start, so maybe offer your first three customers a free article in return for a testimonial – if of course, they like your work!

Once you have built up a good reputation, you can begin to increase your price to a more realistic one.

Webmasters are always on the lookout for good writers, so, if you provide excellent work, you will never be short of work.

If you are good at the 'purple prose' you could offer a service on Valentine's Day writing love poems for lovers to send to their 'other half' or you could even write love letters for those who would love to be romantic but lack any writing skills.

Another great benefit of this type of money making opportunity is that you can work anywhere in the world that you can get an internet connection.

Writing for Magazines

There are thousands of magazines that will pay you for a good article, short story, editorial etc.

For an extensive list of magazines try this link:

http://dir.yahoo.com/news_and_media/magazines

Once you have found a magazine that you think you may be able to write for, go to their website and scroll to the bottom of the home page. This is where you would usually find the submission guidelines link.

If there is no option for submitting your work, send a simple email to the magazine asking for their submission guidelines.

Writing for magazines can be much more lucrative than writing articles for $10 as you could be getting paid $100 to $1000 per piece.

Bonus Method 3

Become a Voiceover Artist

There are four main voiceover categories: commercials, narrations, characterizations and imaging. Which one do you think that you would be most suited to?

Buy yourself a microphone. Use a computer to record and playback for practice and critique.

You should simply keep on practising your interpretation of the material without focusing on how your voice sounds to you.

There are not many people who enjoy listening to a recording of themselves, so ask for an unbiased opinion from a friend.

Produce a demo and put it on to CD. If you are determined to follow this career path and have a bit of cash available to invest in your future, you may consider having a professional demo done.

Remember that your demo is the first thing an agent will hear and you will only get one chance to make a first impression.

Find talent agencies and companies that may use voiceover artists, like video production houses, smaller ad agencies, radio stations. Call or email them to get the name of the right person to contact.

Then send your demo CD with a covering letter and a business card.

If you do not hear anything within a week or two, follow up with a phone call or a letter enquiring if they have received the demo CD.

You could also think about signing with a talent agency or joining an organization of voice over artists but you may be expected to pay a membership fee. Have a look at www.voices.com, they have lots of voice over jobs just waiting for you.

If you are lucky enough to land an assignment, make sure you get a copy of the work, this will serve as a demo CD for the next assignment and should help you to get more work.

My final thoughts:

Spending a few hours each day working one or two of these methods could make you a nice bit of extra cash.

When you begin your new home business it may be a good idea to have a look at

http://www.score.org/about-score

This website can help by showing you where you can get advice and attend networking meetings.

You would probably not be able to buy a second home with your earnings but, if you stick at and put in the work, you should be able to make some extra cash to ease your transition from paid clock watcher to relaxed work at home mom.

I personally, have used all of these methods to earn extra money to finance my bigger projects. It meant that my journey to a sustainable online income was almost entirely paid for by these methods.

OK, so they may not make you instantly rich but you can use the cash earned to provide those little extras for the family, buy domain names, pay for hosting or even pay for outsourcing stuff that is beyond your capabilities etc.

So, make a pledge to yourself to do the work to set up just one of these simple money machines.

Then do it!

I look forward to hearing about your success.

I love to hear about the achievements of others.

Take Action Now!

If you have any questions about anything in this book or if you would like an extensive list of guidelines for magazine submissions send an email to:

ljs@iwantd.com

For a free bonus money making report check out:

www.iwanted.com

If you are interested in sites that allow you to use their images for free or sites that allow you to use their music for free CLICK HERE

www.ingramcontent.com/pod-product-compliance
Lightning Source LLC
Chambersburg PA
CBHW071639170526
45166CB00003B/1362